The Ultimate
MINISTRY TOOL BOX SERIES

How to Start a Clown Ministry

Daniel King

I dedicate this book to Pastors John & Shirley Tasch,
the best children's pastors in the world.

How to Start a Clown Ministry

ISBN: 1-931810-17-6

Copyright: 2014

Daniel King - King Ministries International
PO Box 701113
Tulsa, OK 74170 USA
1-877-431-4276
daniel@kingministries.com
www.kingministries.com

Table of Contents

Introduction

When I was ten years old, my parents became missionaries in the country of Mexico. We packed up our entire family and moved to a foreign nation. In Mexico we began ministering to children in large evangelistic services. Before every service, we ran through the neighborhoods passing out tracts and invitations to the service. One day we discovered that if we dressed up as clowns as we ran through the neighborhoods, many more people would come to the church. The King family had discovered an awesome ministry tool!

Once we arrived at the church with all the children, we were clowns with nothing to do, so we began to perform short, funny skits for the kids. Later we learned how to juggle, ride unicycles, sing, and preach as clowns. The response from the Mexican kids was wonderful; they screamed with laughter every time they saw us.

By the time I was fourteen, American churches began to invite my brother Stephen and I to come minister to their kids. The clowning began to open up many doors of opportunity. Because I was only fourteen and my brother was only ten, many pastors thought we were too young to minister, until they heard about the quality of our presentation.

Stephen and I were led to begin our own ministry called *Clowns for Christ, International*. As kids, we wrote our own brochures, and booked ourselves. Of course, we had lots of support from our parents as we discovered that God uses young people!

As we grew older, we improved our juggling skills (we can pass seven clubs and juggle six balls each) and began to add other innovative ideas to our tool box. Our show contained ventriloquism, stilt-walking, dancing, gymnastics, puppetry, and funny skits. Stephen is gifted musically so we performed our entire show to original music. Every show included a powerful time of teaching, and an altar call.

Literally thousands of children have come to know the Lord through our ministry. Over 100,000 kids have heard the Gospel through our creative presentations. We began to travel internationally and we have ministered in Jamaica, Venezuela, Costa Rica, Russia, France, Germany, Spain, Korea, Sweden, Mexico, and across the United States.

Together we formed the team of Feliz (Spanish for *happy*) and Gozo (Spanish for *joy*). Imagine a fun-filled, high-energy, fast-moving, presentation of the Gospel in a circus extravaganza and you have the Clowns for Christ. Our goal was to be funny, entertaining, and evangelistic.

With over half the world's population fifteen years old or younger, it is vital to reach the next generation. Jesus said, *"Let the little children come to Me and forbid them not, for of such is the kingdom of heaven"* (Mark 10:14).

We believe God wants us to reach the children of the world. To accomplish this we know we can not do it alone. We must reproduce ourselves, so we wrote this book to help you learn how to be

a "Clown for Christ." I pray you use the tools in this book to reach thousands of children.

What is a Clown?

A clown is...

approachable, awkward, amusing, absurd, awesome,

blundering, bumbling,

curious, comical, clever, clumsy,

droll, dandy, daffy,

entertaining, exciting, exotic,

friendly, flighty, flippant, frivolous, fantastic, funny, fun,

good-natured, gawky, gracious, graceful, generous, great,

hilarious, humorous, helpful,

intelligent, inept,

jugglers, jesters, jokers, joyful,

klutzy, kid-like,

laughable, likable, lively,

marvelous, merry-makers,

neat, nice, nonsensical,

outrageous, obliging, outlandish,

preposterous,

quaint,

ridiculous,

silly, sensational, splendid, superb,

tremendous, terrific,

ungraceful, uncoordinated,

valiant, valuable, vaudevillian,

whimsical, witty, wonderful, wacky,

xylophonic,

yakker, yo-yo, yummy,

and zany.

Clowns project a friendly character through exaggeration. They are like a giant cartoon character who suddenly comes to life. The difference between a clown and a comedian is that a comedian says and does funny things, while a clown says or does normal things in a funny way. The mandate of a clown is to spread joy everywhere through actions, words, smiles, and Christlikeness.

Biblical Basis
for Clowning

Throughout the Bible, joy is a characteristic of those who serve God. In God's presence there is a fullness of joy, and we know that the "joy of the Lord" is the source of all of our strength. The second fruit of the spirit is joy. Clowns are tools which can be used to bring happiness and joy to a sad situation. Here are some verses which show the importance of joy in the life of a Christian.

* Nehemiah 8:10 *"The joy of the Lord is my strength."*
* Psalm 35:27 *"Let them shout for joy, and be glad."*
* Psalm 16:11 *"In Thy presence is a fullness of joy."*
* Psalms 66:1 *"Shout with joy to God, all the earth!"*
* Phillipians 4:4 *"Rejoice in the Lord always and again I say rejoice."*
* Psalms 98:4 *"Make a joyful noise unto the Lord."*
* Proverbs 17:22 tells us, *"A merry heart doeth good like a medicine."*

Medical research has proven that those who laugh often are healthier than those who are depressed. Laugher cures both emotional and physical diseases. Clowns are doctors who fill the prescription for laughter.

Christians are commanded in 1 Corinthians 4:10 to become *"fools for Christ's sake."* This means the foolishness of the gospel will confound the wisdom of the world. In other words, Christians should pursue the things of God even if they appear foolish in the eyes of the world. There is no greater fool than a clown. A Christian clown acts as a fool to teach deep spiritual truths. In Greek theater, a white face represented death, but colorful markings were symbolic of life. A clown applies white makeup, which represents death to self, and then the clown adds bright colors to his or her face, which represents a new birth. When a clown puts on makeup and costume, the old character dies, and suddenly the clown is a new being. The parallels to dying to self and resurrecting in Christ are obvious.

The goal of Christian clowning should be the evangelization of the world. Jesus told His disciples they would be fishers of men. Clowning can be used as a big net to catch children. Saint Francis of Assisi once said, "Preach at all times, and when necessary, use words." Clowning enables us to preach about the love of God through our actions. People around the world like to laugh. Most cultures have traditions about "wise fools" who present powerful messages through simple dramatic skills. Clowning can be used to tap into the heartbeat of a culture and to communicate through humor. Entertaining people is a great way to make friends and once you have made a friend, they will listen to your presentation of the gospel.

The moon never shines; it only reflects the light of the sun. What appears to be a shining light is in reality only a reflection. It is impossible for the moon to shine by itself. When a performer shines, it is not because of inherent talents or personal skills, but because he or she is a reflection of the Son of God. Jesus is the Light of the world, and He is the One who enables us to be shining lights. Clowning allows the love of God to shine through your life.

How to Start a Clown Ministry

1. Prayer

Prayer will lay the foundation for your clown ministry. Without prayer, all you will have is a bunch of foolish clowns running around; with prayer, you will have a powerful tool for the Kingdom of God. God answers prayer.

Once there was an elder of a church who owned a parrot. Unfortunately, the only thing the parrot knew how to say was, "Let's kiss! Let's kiss!" Since the elder wanted his parrot to be respectable, he mentioned the problem to his pastor. The pastor told him he had a parrot, too. But, the pastor's bird only said, "Let's pray. Let's pray." So, they decided to put the two birds together in hopes that the first parrot would learn some decent language. When they put them in one cage, the first parrot said, "Let's kiss! Let's kiss!" Immediately, the pastor's bird squawked, "Hallelujah! My prayers have been answered!" The point is that prayer changes things.

2. Give your clown group an identity.

A name is important because it will give your group an identity. McDonald's Restaurants are famous, not because of the quality of their food, but because of the marketing of their name. Here are some

ideas for a creative name for your Clown Ministry.

1. The Comical Christian Clowns
2. The Hilarious High Hoppers
3. The Laugh Pack
4. The Amazing Amusers
5. The A-men Joys (sounds like Almond Joys)
6. Amuse-U Clown Company
7. S.M.I.L.E. Super Ministries In Laughter Evangelism

Here are a couple of ideas for a clown team motto.
1. "Goofy but Godly"
2. "Feed World Humor"

3. Develop a system of organization to run the team.

A system is important so the clown group will not fall apart if some-one leaves. Have regular times of practice and ministry. Perhaps the first Sunday of every month could be "Clown Sunday." Organization involves several elements.

The most important element of organization is leadership. Strong leadership must be in place. Choose someone who passionately loves clowning and who has strong organizational and teaching skills. Recruitment of potential clowns is important. Recruit one or two times each year and then spend quality time training those people. Advertise in your church to find people who are interested in clowning and then ask those people to make a six-month commit-ment to practicing and performing.

Teenagers make great clowns because they have lots of energy and time on their hands to learn skills like juggling, unicycling, and ven-triloquism. However, every group of young people needs a couple of adults to encourage, supervise, and instruct.

Sample job descriptions for the leaders of the typical clown ministry team.

Clown Director

Duties:

1. Provide spiritual leadership.
2. Oversee training sessions.
3. Schedule performances and ministry sessions.
4. Plan rehearsals and creative idea sessions.
7. Notify clowns of rehearsals and performances.

Assistant Director

Duties:

1. Assist the clown director in his responsibilities.
2. Train and develop personnel to perform as clowns.
3. Lead in the development of routines and other performance material.
4. Coordinate and train clowns for skits.
5. Help find costumes for clowns and train them to put on makeup.

Service Coordinator

Duties:

1. Assist the clown director in his responsibilities.
2. Lead a ministry troupe of clowns.
3. Prepare clown troupe for service.
4. Conduct the service as "Master of Ceremonies."
5. Coordinate props and personnel to be present at performances.

Props Coordinator

Duties:

1. Answer to and assist the service coordinator.
2. Coordinate the selection and building of all props.
3. Check out and return all props and accessories.

4. Coordinate music tapes with the sound technician.

5. Prepare stage for performance.

4. Professionalism

Strive to be professional. Makeup, costumes, and good material is important. Our goal is to reach the lost; sometimes this goal forces us to compete with the world's standards of professionalism. If we are going to attract people to Christ, we must not only do our best, we must be the best at what we do. There is no excuse for sloppiness or unprofessional behavior.

5. Look for a need and fill it.

Clowns can attract the attention of both children and adults. Everyone loves to use their imagination and a clown is the perfect vehicle to induce the use of the imagination. In today's sight and sound generation where television is given such prominence, you need something to grab a child's attention. A clown is perfect for this!

On TV, something new is happening every thirty seconds. The colorful enthusiasm of a clown generates excitement and interest in a society which has overdosed on entertainment. Children will allow a clown to enter their world and this opens up doors for ministry. Clown ministry is a great way for Christians to communicate the gospel in a way worldly people can understand it.

Where in the Church can Clowning be Used?

1. Vacation Bible Schools - A clown can provide excitement, making VBS a memorable week for all the kids.

2. Children's Church - Clowns can teach verses, do object lessons, greet kids, perform skits, and do ice breakers.

3. Parks - Passing out balloons in parks is a great way to invite people to come to your church.

4. Parties - Birthday kids often invite unsaved friends from their neighborhood to their birthday parties. This can be a great opportunity for a clown to present a gospel message.

5. Promotions - Promote your church by standing on the street corner and waving.

6. Nursing Homes - Senior citizens are lonely and they love clowns to come and talk with them.

7. Parades - Marching in a parade with a group of clowns from your church can attract families to your church. Try passing out candy with a tract attached.

8. Shopping Malls - These are a great place to meet people but be sure to ask permission first.

9. Training Sessions - Teach what you know about clowning to others.

10. Evangelistic Outreaches - Sending clowns out in the neighborhoods to invite people to a service will greatly increase attendance.

11. Mission Trips - Children around the world love clowns. A clown can communicate the love of God, even if they do not know the language.

12. Worship Service - Clowns can be ushers on a special Sunday, or they can serve communion. If this is done respectfully it can have great impact as the church members see a clown learn about the importance of the sacraments.

13. To meet and greet people arriving at church - Shake hands and wave as people arrive at church. Everyone needs a little bit of the joy of the Lord.

14. Hospitals - Those who are sick need a little bit of encouragement from a clown. Laughter doeth good like a medicine.

Types of
Clown Characters

There are three basic types of clowns. These categories are based on makeup and costume design. Traditionally, there are specific ways in which each clown acts. Many skits are based on interaction between these characters. You should decide on what type of character you want to be, then you should work on your makeup and costume.

The White Face Clown
Makeup - Neat white face with simple, colorful, markings, often outlined with black pencil.
Costume - Elegant jumpsuit or baggy two piece suit, usually has a ruff around the neck, and the color schemes are simple. May wear a skull cap, wig, or hat. Wears gloves. Looks like a cartoon character brought to life. May wear a tuxedo.
Way of Acting - This is the smart clown (at least he thinks he is smart). He is the straight man who sets up comedy situations. He is often highly skilled at some talent. He comes up with plots and thinks of pranks to play on others. He is usually the victim at the end of the skit because of something the auguste clown did to mess up his scheme.

The Auguste Clown (pronounced Ah-goost")

Makeup - Base color for makeup is usually a fleshy tone of pink, orange, or light brown. This clown's mouth and eyes are usually surrounded by white makeup in order to make them stand out. Wears lipstick. Cheeks may be highlighted. The features are larger then the white face clown's features and more exaggerated. Often wears a bright red nose.

Costume - Loose fitting, plaid or printed cloth, suspenders, possibly overalls, multicolored shirt. Large hat, gloves, may wear a colorful suit jacket.

Way of Acting - This is usually the dumber clown. He messes up everything the white face clown tries to do. He misunderstands instructions and forgets how to do things. He is often the victim of pranks but of course, he never really gets hurt.

The Tramp Clown

Makeup - White mouth without lipstick, beard and heavy black eyebrows, red cheeks and nose.

Costume - Old, worn-out clothing with patches and stains. The actual costume is clean but it has been through a lot. Scraggly hair, and gloves with the fingers cut off. May carry a stick with all his possessions tied on or a beat-up briefcase.

Way of Acting - Happy-go-lucky, lazy, bum who does not care about money or who pretends to be rich. He may be unhappy and move slowly or he may a character who tries hard without anything ever seeming to work out.

Developing
Clown Character

Character (kar'ik ter) *The distinctive traits, qualities, attributes, and characteristics of a personality. The pattern of behavior found in an individual.*

If you want to have a clown character, you must develop a personality for your character. When I say "clown character" I am talking about the distinctive way you will act when you are a clown. Your character is your personality, the qualities of your individual self as a clown. Your clown character is different then your own character. When you become a clown, you really are becoming a new person. Your new personality has likes and dislikes, strengths and weaknesses, goals and desires.

Clown character is the single most important element of clowning. Your character is who you are. It is like the flavor in a popsicle, the seasoning in a recipe, and the spice of life. Character adds zest, tang, and kick to who you are.

Your clown character can be an extension or an exaggeration of your normal behavior. Or your clown character can be completely different from the way you typically act. Regardless, a clown with char-

acter is more interesting and memorable then a clown without any distinctive characteristics.

Will your clown character be shy, bashful, and reserved, or will you be outgoing, extroverted, and sociable? Everyone has a character flaw, when these normal character flaws are identified and exaggerated the effect is often humorous. As a clown, what do you like, what do you hate, what are you afraid of, and how do you react in situations?

Here are some adjectives you may use to describe your clown's characteristics.

Happy, Bright, Cultured, Lucky, Witless, Lazy, Sad, Brilliant, Highbrow, Miserly, Silly, Relaxed, Shy, Clever, Learned, Greedy, Flighty, Lethargic, Fearful, Astute, Scholarly, Stingy, Flippant, Lackadaisical, Nervous, Shrewd, Trustworthy, Irritated, Frivolous, Cool, Apprehensive, Thoughtful, Reliable, Angry, Levelheaded, Passionate, Intelligent, Wise, Curious, Irate, Thoughtful, Emotional, Dumb, Powerful, Bizarre, Selfish, Encouraging, Dramatic, Slow, Quick, Witty, Egotistical, Boastful, Romantic, Stupid, Gifted, Punny, Pompous, Bashful, Impractical, Idiotic, Bookish, Satisfied, Self-centered, Reserved, Dreamer

Personality is extremely important. As a clown, you will be remembered and loved for the way you act, not because of what you wear or what tricks you perform. Audiences want to be emotionally involved with you personally. They want to relate to a real being who has strengths and weaknesses. Choose to be a character that the audience can identify with. When they laugh at you, they should really be laughing at themselves.

Character Development WorkSheet

Name: _____

Age: _____

Place of Birth: _____

Did your character go to school? What are your character's hobbies?

_____

What is your favorite sport, book, food, and color?

_____

Is your character rich or poor? What are your character's goals in life?

_____

Are you a whiteface clown, auguste clown, or a character clown?

_____

Describe your appearance. What kind of costume, wig, hat, make-up are you wearing?

_____

_____

_____

Use some adjectives to describe your character. (For example, one could be an intelligent, friendly, outgoing, fun-loving, clown. Or one could be a lazy, dumb, uninterested, sleepy, idle, lethargic clown. Interaction between these two clown types would be great because the first one would be excitedly waving at an audience while the other one would be yawning.)

_____

_____

_____

_____

What are your character's strengths and weaknesses?

_____

Do you carry any special props? (For example, a tramp could carry a broom with a handkerchief tied to one end.)

_____

If your character could live anywhere, where would you live?

_____

Is your character a good Christian, or a work in progress?

_____

How to Apply Clown Make-up

Makeup is an important element of clowning. People identify you by your face and it is what people look at the most. Your makeup should enhance your facial expressions and help you project your feelings from far away. You can buy the items you need for your makeup kit in stores which carry theatrical makeup.

You will need:
1. Clown White grease paint
2. Lining sticks (several colors)
3. Small Make-up brushes
4. Talcum Power (Baby Power)
5. Soft Brush
6. Wet Wipes
7. Damp Sponge
8. Cold Cream or Baby oil
9. Q-tips or cotton balls
10. Eyebrow pencil (Black)
11. Bobby pins or hair clips

Steps

1. Wipe face clean. Make sure all makeup is cleaned off.

2. Push all hair back and pin out of the way.

3. Look in the mirror and study your face. Make faces and see where your muscles move the most. These are the areas of your face that are the most flexible and which you will want to emphasize with color.

4. Put on a thin coat of baby oil or cold cream. Wipe it off. This will help protect your face and make it easier to remove the makeup.

5. Cover the entire face with a thin coat of clown white. Caution: Most beginning clowns put on entirely to much clown white. It should be applied so sparingly that your regular skin color shows through. If you are a white face clown, it looks best if you cover your ears and neck as well as your face.

6. Using your three middle fingers, pat the entire white face repeatedly to work makeup into pores and to give your face a smooth appearance.

7. With a Q-Tip or cotton ball, wipe places clean where you will put color. If you make a mistake, just pat the area with the white and try again.

8. Powder the entire face with a powder-filled sock. Powder liberally. If your face feels sticky, powder some more. This powder will protect your makeup from sweat, rain, and grabbing fingers.

9. Gently brush off excess powder with a soft brush.

10. Apply the colored makeup with the brushes. Keep the markings small and neat rather then large and grotesque. The best colors to use are red and blue. Keep the smile within your laugh lines, if your smile extends from ear to ear it will make you look like a Halloween pumpkin which is scary. Keep all hearts, stars, and lines small rather then huge. After markings are complete, powder, then brush off the excess powder.

11. Use black lining sticks or eyebrow pencil to outline nose and mouth with a thin black line. Powder as before.

12. After the entire face has been painted, powdered, and brushed, gently blot with a damp sponge. This will remove the extra powder, make your colors stand out, and leave your face feeling comfortable.

13. Do not worry about goofing. If you make a mistake, just wipe it off with baby oil and do it again. It will take several times before you get it the way you want it.

14. To remove: try some cold cream or baby shampoo followed by soap and water.

Creative Costumes

Clown costumes can be as simple as a colorful T-shirt and a pair of overalls, or it can be as complicated as a specially tailored tuxedo. You can find great clown costumes in second-hand stores and at garage sales, or you can find someone to sew a costume to fit your personal preferences. Look for bright, funny looking clothes. Find a funny hat or wear a wig. Take something plain and decorate it with big buttons, suspenders, bows, collars, and anything else you can find. Look for patterns from sewing stores.

Our clown characters have developed their own distinctive costumes over the years. Feliz wears a rainbow colored suit with a bright red hat and matching shoes. In order to tailor the suit, we bought normal patterns at a sewing store and made a pair of pants and a vest out of brightly colored cloth. Gozo wears baggy overalls with a colorful shirt. He wears a blue wig and a funny little hat. Another character we use is a tramp named Flojo (*Lazy* in Spanish). He wears a red and black checkered bathrobe and matching pants. He also carries a broom around with him everywhere he goes. Each of these costumes is simple, yet funny looking.

Tips to remember when making clown costumes.

* Pockets are an asset - The bigger your pockets are, the more stuff you can store in them. Pockets hold stickers, props, balloons, and candy. Some pockets can be big and visible on the outside of your costume, but some pockets should be hidden where children can not get into them or see the surprises you have stored.

* Make your suit user-friendly - Baggy one-piece suits are great... until you have to go to the bathroom. Make sure you include a zipper. If you are going to be clowning in hot weather, design your suit to be cool so you do not burn up.

* Costumes should always be kept neat - Costumes must always be kept clean and pressed. Appearance is of the upmost importance. Even a tramp clown's costume which may be designed to look dirty should be kept clean at all times.

* Make your costume durable - You will be rolling somersaults, riding unicycles, and performing extensively. If your costume is made of fragile material, it will tear and wear out quickly.

*Add accessories for variety - Hats, scarves, gloves, suspenders, neckties, and miscellaneous props can change the look and feel of a clown. People wear different clothes for different occasions, why can't clowns? By changing hats, the same clown can play several different characters in a skit.

Clown Props

Props are the tools of a clown. You can use them to attract attention, to entertain, and to teach a lesson. Here are several different categories of props.

1. Invisible Props
Bring your mime skills and invent your own on the spot props. For example, try to start a game of invisible baseball with some kids. Mime the wind-up, the pitch, the hit, and the catch.

Try passing out invisible balloons. These can be just as satisfying to children as real balloons because the real entertainment value comes from how you relate to the children. Search your pockets and discover an invisible balloon, pretend like it is real and stretch it out, then blow it up, tie a knot, and attach a string. By slowly letting your arm rise, it will appear that the balloon is filled with helium. Let it pull you into the air until you are standing on your tip toes. A fight between you and the balloon could ensue until you let the balloon go or pop it with a pin. Congratulations, you just entertained a bunch of kids for five minutes.

2. Hats
Everything you carry around can be turned into an impromptu prop. For example, a hat can be a best friend, an enemy, a roof over your head, a steering wheel, a toy, an obstacle, a handkerchief, an offering bucket, a trusty weapon, a pacifier, a symbol of wealth, a symbol of poverty, a pillow, and old friend, and much more.

3. Musical props
Kids love to sing so you can use kazoos, harmonicas, guitars, tambourines, and accordions.

4. Giant Cell Phone
A blow-up cell phone is funny, especially if you imitate all the people who pretend to be important while they are talking on a cell phone. Plus, the blow-up phone gets lots of free air time.

5. Giant props
Giant comb, giant flyswatters and fly, giant baby bottles, etc.

6. Puppets
Find some furry little animal puppets and put them in a shoe box. Cut a hole in the back of the shoe box so your hand can make the puppet come alive. Little kids love to pet the animals.

7. Water guns
Especially on hot days, kids love to get wet. Hold shoot outs and play games with water guns.

8. Juggling props
Balls, clubs, rings, knives, torches, cigar boxes, unicycles, stilts, scarves, diabolos, shaker cups, special sticks, king rings, rubber chickens, almost anything can be juggled.

Basics of Comedy

What is it that makes some things funny, and other things not funny? What makes the difference between a laughing audience and a bored one? Here are some of the different elements which can create comedy.

Misunderstanding
Some comedy occurs when one clown misunderstands the instructions of another clown. This creates comedy because the clown who gave the instructions does not notice that the other clown misunderstood. Only the audience understands what the original instructions were, and what caused the misunderstanding.

For example, there is a famous clown skit where one clown decides to teach another clown how to do a magic trick. He instructs him to find a yellow bandana. Instead, the other clown rushes off to find a yellow banana. The humor comes when the instructions for the magic trick include folding the bandana several times and then squishing it into one hand. Of course, the first clown can do it easily because he has a real bandana in his hands, but the second clown makes a huge mess with his banana. At the end, the bandana disappears, but the banana is all over the place.

Deliberate Interference

If one clown is deliberately trying to mess up something the other clown is doing, it is funny, especially if he does not know what is wrong.

A great example of this would be when one clown is trying to give a serious speech to the audience. The second clown keeps peeking out from behind a curtain. When the audience laughs, the serious clown turns around trying to find out why they are laughing, but the interfering clown ducks back behind the curtain. The longer this happens, the funnier it gets. When the serious clown spins one way, the other clown is peeking out the other side of the curtain. Finally, the silly clown is caught and a romping chase ensues.

Slapstick Violence

The term "slapstick" comes from the old black and white movie days. Performers would use a special stick to hit each other; every time the stick hit something, it would sound like a slap. For some reason, people think it is funny when other people are beat up. However, violence done willy-nilly is rarely funny. It is important to have a reason to engage in some slapstick.

For example, when the Three Stooges hit one another, it usually begins for a reason. Perhaps one of the Stooges made a mistake or said something stupid and the others feel compelled to punish him. Once one Stooge is hit, it becomes necessary for the other Stooge to hit back. They poke each other in the eyes, and bop heads for a while before they get back to the business at hand.

Characterization

The best comedy comes because of a quirk in someone's character. When a clown has a consistent character, it is easy to create comedy

using that character.

For example, the famous radio comedian Jack Benny spent years developing his character as a stingy, old, miser who carefully guarded every cent he had. His money was kept in a huge safe underneath his basement, protected by a moat with alligators, a guard, and hundreds of locks and bolts. On one radio program, Jack was walking home at night, when a thief came up behind him, put a gun in his back and said, "Your money or your life!" There followed one of the longest pauses on radio ever, over forty-five seconds. The robber whispered it again, "Your money or your life!" Jack replied, "Hold on, I'm still thinking." The audience laughed for almost two minutes.

This is a joke that would have been mildly funny if anyone else would have said it, but because of Jack Benny's character which he had carefully cultivated for many years, the joke brought the house down.

Suspense
If an audience suspects something is going to happen, the suspense of waiting for it to happen creates comedy. Imagine, a clown comes out on stage and eats a banana. Before he leaves he throws the banana skin down in the middle of the stage. Then, one at a time, clowns rush across the stage carrying large loads. Everyone in the audience is holding their breath waiting for someone to trip and fall on the banana. The more suspense, the funnier it gets. Finally, there is a lull in the rushing about and slowly an old clown walks out with a broom and sweeps up the banana and walks off. This sudden release of tension will cause the audience to laugh.

Repetition
A running gag gets funnier and funnier the more times it is repeated.

A running gag gets funnier and funnier the more times it is repeated.
A running gag gets funnier and funnier the more times it is repeated.

At the beginning of a show, a clown brings out a bucket and plants a seed. Periodically during the show, he brings the bucket back out on the stage. The first time, the audience sees that a tree has begun to grow. Each time he returns, the tree gets taller and taller. Finally, at the end, the tree is so big the clown can barely carry it. Just the repetition creates humor.

Word Plays
Some say the highest form of humor is the pun; others say puns are the lowest form of humor. Regardless, whether people laugh or groan, puns and word plays are funny. The English language has so many words with two or more meanings, it is easy to come up with some great jokes.

Funny Situations
A funny situation creates comedy because the audience sympathizes with the performer. For example, if a clown is trying to catch a fly, the audience can relate because everyone has tried to catch a fly at one time or another. When the fly swatter does not work, the clown decides to use a long strip of sticky fly paper. As he tries to catch the fly, objects get stuck to the paper, and eventually, the clown gets completely tangled up in the sticky mess. A great ending to this situation could have the fly come and land on top of the tangled clown.

Impromptu humor
Impromptu humor is always loved by the audience. Making use of accidents and mistakes to create comedy requires the performer to think quickly on his feet. Utilizing the resources at hand to produce a funny situation is loved by all.

One day we were outside in a park doing a show when the wind picked up. As our stuff was blowing away, Feliz shouted, "Look, our props are being blown away!" Gozo retorted, "Just like our audience." Since this was totally impromptu humor the audience loved it.

At the same show, Feliz brought up a volunteer. The volunteer's hair was sticking up, so Gozo found some water to plaster the hair back down. A comic chase scene ensued which ended with Gozo getting wet. This scenario was so funny that we have now included it in other shows.

How to Use Pantomime

Often a clown will use pantomime to communicate with the audience. Miming is a great asset when you cannot be heard or when you are in a foreign country where you do not know the language. Make your movements bigger than life. A great way to discover how to mime is to watch cartoon characters and imitate their actions. Here are some ways to convey ideas without using words.

Happiness: Smile big, turn cartwheels, clap your hands, and jump up and down.

Sadness: Frown, sob, and blow your nose into a handkerchief.

Impatience: Look at your watch, tap your foot, fidget, squirm, and put your hands on your hips.

Bad smell: Hold your nose, and use a clothespin to pinch your nose shut.

Fear: Tremble, hide behind something, make your teeth chatter, and bite your fingernails.

Pride: Puff out your chest, put your nose in the air, and snap imaginary suspenders.

Anger: Shake your fist at someone, jump up and down, and hit your head against something.

Falling in Love: Put your hand inside your shirt and make it look

like your heart is beating fast, let your tongue hang out, sigh, and draw a big heart with your hands.

Exhaustion: Breathe heavily, hold on to something to prop yourself up, wobble around in circles, and finally fall down.

Running: Run in place, move your arms up and down really fast, huff and puff, and pause as if exhausted.

Pain: Rub the sore spot with your hands, stagger around in a circle, yell, and if you are hit by an object, fall in the opposite direction.

Now, create funny and interesting ways your character would act in these situations.

You are

> ... meeting a new friend.
> ...picking a flower.
> ...walking through a crowd of people.
> ...performing a magic trick for a group of kids.
> ...shaking another clown's hand.
> ...reacting when another clown plays a trick on you.
> ...drinking a glass of water.
> ...asked to fill a bucket with water.
> ...praying.
> ...playing a sport you have never heard of before.
> ...stuck in the rain.
> ...studying for a big test.
> ...walking a dog or walking an elephant.
> ...eating a piece of candy.
> ...taking tickets at the door of a theater.
> ...cleaning up the house.
> ...cooking.

Remember, you are not limited to using pantomime; spoken words are often the best way to communicate, however, miming an action often gets an idea across better than words can. A picture can be worth a thousand words.

Balloon Animal Fun

Kids love balloons. There is something about the colorful, squeaky nature of balloons which appeals to children. Not only are balloon animals fun to make, they are also easy to learn.

What type of balloon should I use?

Use a 260E balloon. The "2" means that it is three inches in diameter, the "60" means that when it is fully inflated, it is sixty inches long. The "E" means the balloon is easy to blow up. One of the best companies who sells balloons is called "Qualatex." You can usually find these balloons at a local party store.

How do I blow up a balloon?

The easiest way to blow up a balloon is by using a pump (also known as cheating). Electric pumps and handheld inflators both work. But, eventually you will want to know how to blow one up with your mouth.

When blowing up a balloon with your mouth it is important to use the proper technique or your cheeks will get sore. First, stretch the balloon. The more you stretch it, the easier it will be to blow up. Second, pinch the balloon one inch from the open end. Begin blow-

ing air into the balloon. Be sure to blow from your lungs, not from your cheeks. As you blow, slowly pull the air into the balloon by stretching the balloon away from you. A bubble of air should pop up in the end of the balloon. Third, take a deep breath and blow up the entire balloon.

This process will be difficult at first. The first time you try, you may only be able to blow up one or two balloons. But keep practicing and it will become easy. Even once you become good, you may still want to carry a pump around with you in case you have to blow up balloons for hundreds of children at one time.

Dog

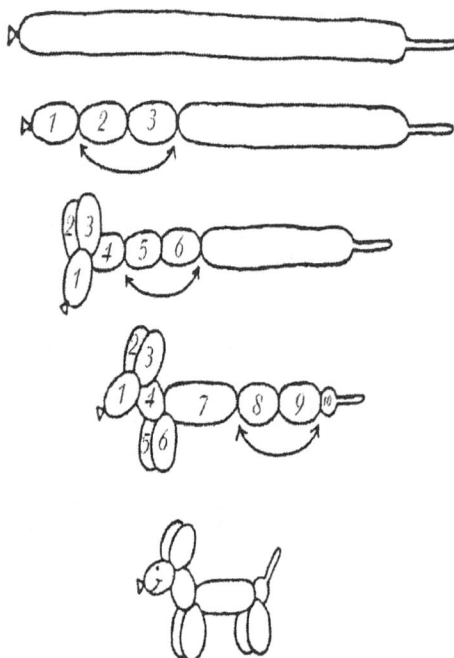

Twist a 2" bubble near the end where you blew up the balloon. Hold on to the first bubble and twist two more the same size. Twist the three bubbles together. This forms the nose and the two ears of the dog. Twist a neck, now twist two 3" bubbles in the balloon and twist them together. These bubbles form the front legs of the dog. Make a 5" body for the dog and then twist two more 3" bubbles for the back legs. Twist the back legs together and the leftover balloon is the tail of the dog.

Giraffe

The giraffe is just like the dog, except you give him a long neck and almost no tail.

Horse

The horse is made of ten bubbles just like the dog and the giraffe. Make the ears small and give him a medium neck and a long tail.

Hat

A hat only requires one twist. Measure the head of the child and comment on how smart they must be. Twist the balloon in that spot and you should have a fish-shaped hat. Put it on the head of the child.

Sword

To make a sword, fold a balloon in threes. It should look like a "z" shaped figure. Grip the entire "z" and twist all three parts at one time. This forms the handle and guard in one easy twist. If you hold the sword by the blade, it looks like a cross.

Creative Balloon Idea #1: If you do not have room to carry a bunch of props around with you for dramas, try to create the props you need by inventing new balloon figures. For example, one time we wanted to teach a group of children about the armor of God, but we did not want to carry a helmet, a shield, a sword, and all the other parts of the armor. So, we figured out how to create each piece of the Armor of God using only animal balloons.

Creative Balloon Idea #2: Try using balloons to tell the story of Noah and the Ark by making two of every kind of animal you know how to make.

Creative Balloon Idea #3: Blow up several balloons and label them as different kinds of diseases. Hand them to volunteers to hold. For

example, one balloon could say "Cancer," another one "Headache," and a third one "Heart attack." Put a pin in the end of your Bible and explain how the Word of God destroys sickness. Quote a verse about healing and hit the balloon with your Bible. The pin in the end makes the balloon pop. Jesus destroys "Cancer!" Repeat this process for the other sicknesses.

Creative Balloon Idea #4: Make a balloon dog and have him do tricks. If you make the do a really long tail, you can use it like a leash and control the dog. Sit up. Roll over (Spin the dog over and over.) Jump. Bark (Rub your finger along the side of the dog and it will squeak.) Spin. Fly (Balloon dogs can do this.) Play dead (Stomp on the balloon. This is usually the end of the routine.)

What to say when the balloon pops.
1. Put your hand over your heart and say, "May he rest in pieces."
2. Pick up the broken balloon and hand to a child and say, "I made you a worm."
3. Say, "Oh, no. My balloon committed suicide.
4. Pretend like you have been shot.
5. Hold up the balloon and say, "This is why a balloon dog should never have pierced ears."
6. Cry and hold a funeral.

How to Juggle

I am going to teach you the easiest way to learn how to juggle. The best way to learn is to break the process of juggling down into its smallest pieces, and then to master each individual part. After all the pieces are learned, the whole becomes easy. This step-by-step process will have you juggling in no time at all.

Step 1: Pick up one juggling ball. Imagine that there is a window frame in front of you. The frame is about 3" wide and the top of it is about 3" above your head. Throw the ball from hand to hand. Every throw should hit the top of your imaginary window frame and stay within the horizontal constraints of the window. Throw the ball from left to right about ten times. It is absolutely easy.

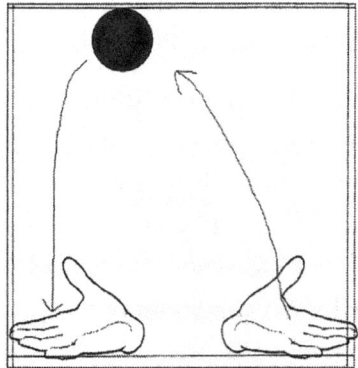

Step 2: Pick up a second juggling ball. Hold one in your left hand and one in your right. Throw the right hand ball first. When it peaks (or hits the top of the window frame), throw the second ball. There

is a huge temptation to hand the left hand ball over to the right hand, but this is cheating. Instead of handing it over, throw the second ball to the same height the first ball went to and then catch it in your right hand.

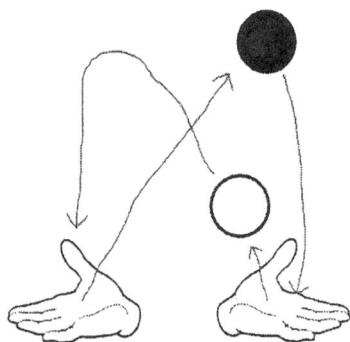

The sequence goes like this: Throw right hand ball, right hand ball peaks, throw left hand ball, left hand ball peaks, catch the first throw in your left hand, catch the second ball in your right hand. Congratulations, you have now completed an exchange. The balls have changed hands. Do this ten times in a row, then try throwing the ball in you left hand first. The exact same thing happens, but you start with the other hand first.

Step 3: Learn how to pick up from a drop. Get used to it, you will probably be dropping quite a bit. That was a joke. Slowly bend down, pick up the ball and try again.

Step 4: Pick up a third ball. Three balls is no harder then two balls. Hold two balls in your right hand. Throw the first one, when it peaks, throw the ball in your left hand. Up until now, you have done the same thing as you did with two balls, except now you do not stop. When the second ball peaks, throw the third ball. Catch all three balls. You end with two balls in your left hand and one in your right.

This is called a jug. It is one part of a juggle. The right hand throws, the left hand throws, the right hand throws, then the left hand catches, the right hand catches, and finally the left hand catches the last ball.

Step 5: Now, instead of just catching the balls, try throwing them back up into the air again. The rhythm goes like this: right, left, right, left, right, etc. Every time a ball peaks, throw the next one into the air. Keep all the balls within the window frame.

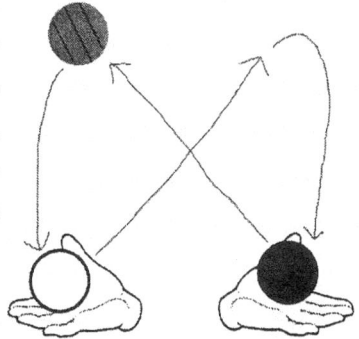

One common problem is when you throw the balls too far forward which causes you to run after them. Solve this by controlling the throws.

Another problem is when the balls speed up faster than you can catch them. This is caused when you do not throw the balls high enough. Keep hitting the top of the imaginary window frame with every ball.

Note: It is easy to learn how to juggle. Every single person who thinks they can learn, will be able to learn to juggle. It is only the people who think they are uncoordinated who never learn this art.

Fun Variations on the Three Ball Cascade

- One Ball High: In the middle of juggling, throw one ball twice as high as normal and catch it when it comes down and continue juggling. For comic effect you can do this repeatedly and hiccup every time the ball goes high. Or after throwing the ball high, grab the bottom hem of your shirt and pull it straight out from your stomach, when the ball comes down, use your shirt as a trampoline to bounce the ball back into the air!

- Over the Shoulder: Throw one ball over your shoulder.

- Behind the Back: Throw one ball behind your back.

- Under the Arm: Catch a ball and move your arm under your other arm before throwing the ball back into the cascade. Try this continuously using the same ball under both arms.

- Under the Leg: Throw one ball under your leg. Try alternating your throws under your left leg and right leg as fast as you can.

- Off the Knee: Bounce ball off your knee. For a variation, juggle two balls in one hand and hold on to the ball as you bounce it off your knee multiple times.

- Off the Elbow: Bounce ball off your elbow.

- Off the Head: Bounce ball off your head.

- Off the Foot: Work in all the hacky-sack moves you know.

- Two in one hand: Juggle two balls in one hand. Meanwhile, your other hand is holding a ball with nothing to do. Try waving with the free hand, wipe your forehead, or spin your free hand around your head a couple of times to get laughs.

- Columns: Throw two in one hand as columns and the third ball goes up and down in your other hand by itself.

- Three in one hand: This trick takes lots of work.

- Over the top: Instead of throwing underneath the other balls, throw one ball back and forth over the top of the other balls.

- In a Circle: When most people try to learn how to juggle, they try this pattern. Only throw with your dominant hand and use your subordinate hand to pass the balls over to your dominant hand.

- Claw the balls: Turn one hand upside down and claw the balls as they come down.

- Ball Bounce: Bounce the ball off the floor and keep juggling when it rebounds. Next, learn to bounce all the balls off the floor repeatedly in a cascade pattern.

- Juggle Four Balls

Four balls is simply juggling two balls in each hand. Practice juggling two balls in one hand, then practice juggling two balls in the other hand. When both hands are competent with juggling two balls, try juggling two balls in each hand at the same time. It's that easy!

- Juggle Ice Cubes: A very cool trick.

- Juggle Apples: Juggle two in one hand for a while and take a bite of the third apple; even busy jugglers have to eat sometime.

- Juggle anything not nailed down: Anything that can flip, spin, or be picked up can be juggled, use your imagination to discover objects that are funny to juggle.

Funny Routine Idea

Feliz and Gozo often challenge each other to a contest. Feliz does a juggling trick first, then Gozo tries to perform the same feat. Invariably, Gozo does the trick wrong. For example, if Feliz does off the knee, Gozo tries to do the same trick but he holds on to the ball and moves his hand up and down off his knee several times. The audience loves it when Gozo messes up every trick. Feliz keeps getting more and more angry that Gozo is not performing the tricks properly.

Lessons from the Art of Juggling

For centuries juggling has been popular. In every culture and in every time period, there have been jugglers who entertained people by the seemingly effortless tossing of miscellaneous objects into the air. What has been the enduring appeal of throwing knives, clubs, balls, rings and torches into the air? Perhaps the appeal comes from the desire of every human to be able to manipulate multiple priorities at one time.

There is much one can learn from the process of juggling. Juggling is a metaphor for life, especially for busy life here in the United States. Everyone struggles to keep things up in the air. Between children, work, social activities, meetings, hobbies, and the need for another dollar, there is a bunch of stuff to juggle. There is always several important things to do and choices must be made. It seems like something is always up in the air.

Learning to juggle is like growing up. The best way to learn how to juggle is to begin with one ball and to master its flight pattern. This is like a baby who has just been born. He only thinks of one thing, food. A baby has no responsibilities and his existence is carefree. But then the child goes to kindergarten and suddenly another ball is thrown into the mix. Now the child must think about school. For years he learns to handle this new responsibility. Then when the child turns sixteen, another ball which needs to be juggled is tossed in his direction in the form of a car. Later, a job needs to be juggled along with a dating relationship. By the time the typical person hits the age of twenty-one, he or she may be juggling a dozen different priorities. Life is the delicate interweaving of multiple responsibilities.

Jugglers learn to perform amazing tricks by breaking the trick down into its smallest parts, and working on each aspect of the trick until it is flawless. No one wakes up one day juggling seven balls. It requires time, effort, and lots of practice. Learning to handle life is the same. The more balls you are juggling, the more discipline and concentration is required. You can achieve the impossible by breaking it up into bite-sized pieces.

All too often, the pattern falls apart. Drops happen. Everyone has dropped the ball at some time in life. Perhaps it was the missed meeting, the forgotten paper, or the lack of study for a test; everyone has made mistakes. But juggling offers a great example for those who drop. If you drop, pick up the ball and try again. Jugglers say, "If you are not dropping, you are not learning anything new." This is because a drop shows that the juggler is pushing the limits of his ability. A pattern without drops is a pattern the juggler is comfortable with and he is not learning anything. Remember, there is no great reward without great risks. At times, you may drop a ball, but pick it back up and appreciate the fact that you are challenging yourself. Push the envelope of your skill level. If you are not making mistakes, you may not be learning anything. Everyone drops the ball occasionally; it is important to pick the ball back up and to keep trying.

Practice makes perfect. Failure is only failure if you fail to learn from your mistakes. Every miss can teach you something. Persistence pays off. Practice is the key to learning how to do anything.

Have faith in yourself. If you never take a chance, you will never improve yourself. Have fun in everything you do. Do not compare yourself against other people; compare yourself against what you

know your potential is. Maintain a desire to learn and to do something new.

There is a feeling of utter satisfaction which comes when one is juggling five balls. It is an achievement comparable to graduating. Some things in life only come through an investment of time. If it was handed to you on a silver platter it would be worthless. There is no way to cheat when learning how to juggle. You will only be as

good as the amount of time you practice. Remember, there are no great rewards without great effort.

A juggling pattern is a thing of beauty because it is organized and structured. Yet there are an infinite number of variations to every pattern. Strive to make your life organized, but make time for variety.

Our lives are like the ultimate juggling pattern. Fortunately, our lives are in the hands of a master juggler. God holds each of His children in the palms of His hands. If at times it feels like we are being thrown through the air, be assured that God will cushion our landing. If we take the wrong flight path and fall, God will pick us back up and throw us to the proper place in His plan. Juggling is fun and so is life; enjoy it!

Juggling Skits

Jesus Rose From the Dead - Juggle two bean bags and a bouncy ball. Talk about all the different types of religions in the world. For example, about 2,500 years ago, there was a man named Buddha who started a religion called Buddhism. Everyone said Buddha was a good man and they said we should follow his ways, but 2,500 years ago, Buddha died (throw one of the beanbags in the air and watch as it hits the floor). About 1,400 years ago, there was another man named Mohammed who came up with a set of rules to live by. His religion is called Islam. Everyone said Mohammed was a prophet and a good man, but 1,400 years ago, Mohammed died (throw up the second beanbag and watch as it plops on the ground). But there was a third man named Jesus. He was both God and man. Jesus claimed to know the way to get to heaven. Two thousand years ago, Jesus died (throw the bouncy ball up into the air), but on the third day, Jesus Christ rose from the dead (catch the ball as it bounces back up). Jesus is still alive today (hold up the ball), unlike the leaders of these other religions (look at the two beanbags that are still on the floor).

Juggling Fleas - If you can not juggle for real, try juggling invisible fleas. There is no limit to the amount of fleas you can juggle or to the

tricks you can perform, not to mention the fun of trying to find our trained fleas in the hair of audience members. At the end of the act, make sure you applaud really loud for your flea troupe, thus squishing them. Wipe them off on your pants and make gross faces.

Balancing Broomsticks - Learning how to balance a broomstick on your hand is simple. All you have to do is keep your eyes focused on the top of the broom and your hand will automatically adjust to keep the stick in balance. Try to maintain the balance on only one finger or try keeping the end of the broom balanced on the tip of a writing pen. Both of these are just as easy as a normal balance but they look harder to audiences. A slightly more difficult balancing trick is to keep the broom steady on your chin.

Teaching: After you have learned how to balance a broomstick, there is a great object lesson you can use with the skill. The broom only remains balanced when your eyes are on the top of it; as soon as you get distracted and look away from the top of the broom, it will fall down. In order for life to be kept in balance, our eyes must focus on Jesus. As soon as we remove our eyes from Jesus, our lives will fall apart. Keep your eyes on Jesus and your life will remain in good balance. Demonstrate this truth by balancing the broom and then suddenly taking your eyes off the top and focusing them on the floor, the broom will fall every time. Finish this teaching by saying, "If you look up, you see Jesus; if you look down, you see defeat (da feet!).

Sleight of Hand

The French Drop

This is a simple way to make any small object like a coin or a ball disappear. First, hold the coin in your left hand between the thumb and the pointing finger. The palm of your left hand is facing up. With the palm of your right hand facing down, reach towards the coin. Wrap your right hand completely around the coin. Now you are still holding the coin between the fingers of your left hand and your right hand is wrapped around the coin with your right thumb underneath the coin. The audience cannot see the coin. Drop the coin from between your left fingers into your left palm. Now, close your right hand tight and move it away from your left hand. Your eyes follow your moving right hand.

It looks like you have taken the coin into your right hand but in reality the coin is still in your left hand. Hold your right hand above your head and look at it. While you are doing this, you can slip the coin in your left hand into your pocket because everyone will look where your eyes are looking. Slowly open the fingers of your right fist. The coin is gone!

You can use this trick to illustrate how God makes our sins completely disappear. Or you can use it to show how Peter escaped from prison. Or you can just use it to entertain young people.

The Disappearing Napkin
This is a trick that can be done for one person or for an entire audience. Invite five people up on stage and tell them that you are going to teach them how to make a napkin disappear. Give each of your helpers a napkin (or the whole audience) and instruct them to do whatever you do.

First, tell them to shake out their napkin. Then tell them to place one corner of the napkin in their left hand. Now, have them bunch their napkins up into their hand. Squish it up until the entire napkin is bundled into a little ball in your left hand. Fourth, ask them to pull a little corner out of their hands. (Up until now, you have been doing the same thing you instructed your helpers to do, but now you secretly do something different. You have had a small corner already torn from another napkin hidden behind the napkin everyone has seen in your hand. Instead of pulling the real corner out, you pull the fake corner out of your fist. After you do this, reach into your fist and remove the tightly bunched up napkin with your right hand. Hide the napkin in the palm of your right hand. No one will know it is there because you keep the back of your right hand towards the audience and because they still think they can see the corner of your napkin sticking out of your left fist.)

Tell your helpers to reach into their pockets and to pull out some imaginary dust. When you demonstrate, you reach into your right pocket and leave the bunched up napkin there. Pull out the imaginary dust and sprinkle it on the napkin. Since this makes the corner of your napkin dirty you are going to have to tear it off. Tell your

helpers to tear off the corner of the napkin that is sticking out of their fists. When you tear off your corner, your hand is completely empty but the assistants still have their napkin in their hands.

Tell them to lift their hand high above their heads and slowly rub them together. Say, "If you've done the trick right, your napkin should have disappeared." Then show them that your napkin disappeared. Of course, their napkins fall out of their hands, and the whole audience has no idea where your napkin went. Smile, and them your helpers that they must not have obeyed your instructions very well. Use this to teach about how important it is to listen to God, and to obey each of His instructions.

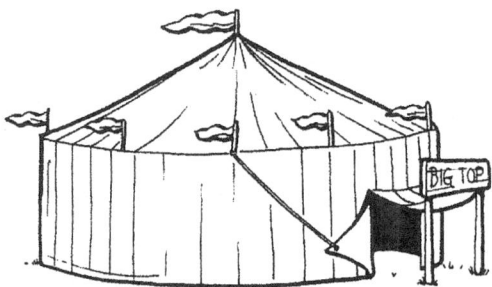

Clown Skits

The best material for Christian clown skits comes straight from the Bible. There are so many good stories and ideas right in the Word of God. One of my favorite places to start is in the parables of Jesus. Each of His stories can easily be adapted to being performed by clowns and of course, they all make a great point.

Clown Skit #1: The Good Neighbor

Here is a skit adapted from the story of the Good Samaritan. The story is found in Luke 10:25-37 and is taken from the New International Clown Version (NICV)

Characters: Whiteface clown, Robbers, Priest, Levite, Good Samaritan, Donkey, Innkeeper, Narrator

Props: Bag of candy, bats or balloons for robbers, bandages

Narrator: *A clown was going down from Jerusalem to Jericho...*
A white face clown, carrying a large bag of candy and is proud of himself walks out on stage.

...when he fell into the hands of robbers. Several tramp or auguste clowns jump out from behind a bush and beat up the white face clown. Use a lot of slapstick comedy.

They stripped him of his nice clothes, beat him up, took his candy and left him for half-dead. The robbers take the candy and run away.

A priest happened to be going down the same road, and when he saw the clown, he passed by on the other side of the road. A clown walks by quoting Luke 10:27 in a religious voice, "Thou shalt love the Lord thy God with all thy heart, and with all thy soul, and with all thy..." The priest notices the hurt man and freaks out. He starts to scream and yell that he cannot stand the sight of blood. The priest stays as far away as possible from the hurt clown and he starts to inch by on the other side of the road. As soon as he gets past the hurt clown the priest regains his composure and starts with the verse again. "...and with all thy mind, and with all thy strength, and thy neighbor as thyself."

So too, a Levite, when he came to the place and saw him, passed by on the other side. Another clown comes by. This clown is singing a song, "This is My commandment that you love one another, that your joy may be full. That your joy may be full. That your joy may be full..." He sees the hurt clown and keeps on singing the song. He even sings a little bit to the clown, but he also passes by on the other side of the road.

But a Samaritan, as he traveled came to where the clown was: and when he saw him he took pity on him. He went to him and bandaged his wounds, pouring on oil and wine. A Good Samaritan clown comes on stage leading a donkey (Be sure he makes some donkey sounds, the louder the better.) When he sees the hurt clown, he immediately takes pity. The clown gets some bandages off his donkey

and starts bandaging the hurt clown's arm. He finishes bandaging the arm and it stays sticking up in the air. The clown is confused. He pushes the arm down and the other arm pops up. He pushes it down and a leg flies up. The clown gets mad. He leans over and pushes the leg down. Both arms fly up and smack the clown. He falls down. When he stands back up, he picks up the hurt clown and then he notices he dropped a bandage. He leans down to pick up the bandage and drops the clown. He turns around and he cannot figure out what happened to the hurt clown. Finally, he notices the clown is laying, groaning at his feet.

Then he put the clown on his own donkey... When he picks the clown back up and puts him on the donkey, the donkey groans and collapses.

...took him to an inn and took care of him. The next day he took out two pieces of candy and gave them to the innkeeper, "Look after him," he said, "and when I return, I will reimburse you for any extra expenses you may have." The donkey takes the white face clown to an innkeeper and the Good Samaritan searches his pockets until he finds two pieces of candy to give the innkeeper.

Clown Skit #2: The Bridge
Characters: Five Clowns (who represent mankind)
    Jesus
    God

Props: Two chairs, rope, sling shot

Stage: God and Jesus are on one side of the stage and the clowns are on the other side. In between them are two chairs set about three feet apart. The space between the chairs represents the great chasm of sin which separates mankind from God.

Narrator: *For many years, mankind has attempted to find a way to get to God. You see, sin (the wrong things we do) separates us from God. Lying, cheating, stealing, and disobedience prevent us from knowing God. Mankind has tried many different ways to get across this wide separation. Sin is like a ditch or a chasm; it is a huge gulf between us an God. Some people think they can get to God if they do enough good things; some think they can get to God if they are rich; some people try to get to God through knowledge. Let's watch as some people try to get to God.*

Action: The scene begins with the five clowns trying to get across the gap between them and God. They gather together in a circle and talk using gestures about how they are going to try to get across. Each clown has an idea and tries it. Each time the other clowns help out and then look disappointed when the method does not work.

The first clown stands up on one chair and begins to get ready to jump across. He prepares to jump, 1-2-3, he falls backwards off the chair and the other clowns catch him. It is not possible to jump across.

The second clown pulls out a long rope, lays it down on the floor and pretends to walk on a tightrope. The clown tries to throw the rope across the ditch, but there is nothing on the other side to catch the end. It is impossible to walk across on a rope.

The third clown tries to crawl under the chair but this clown gets stuck and the other clowns have to pull him free. It is impossible to crawl to God.

The fourth clown pulls out a huge sling shot (the bigger, the better). He is going to try to fly across. He asks the other clowns to hold the ends and he sits in the middle of the sling shot. Someone pulls it back, back, back, and then the end is released. Instead of sending the

clown flying over the gap, the sling shot smacks him in the rear and he falls down. It is impossible to shoot someone over.

The fifth clown stands up on the near chair and pretends to have wings. She flaps her arms but nothing happens. She flaps harder and harder but of course, nothing happens. It is impossible to fly over the gap.

Narrator: *It is impossible for mankind to reach God on his own. Nothing we can do will help us get to God. Every plan man has tried failed. But, wait.... I think God has a plan.*

Action: God and Jesus begin talking together. Using motions, God communicates how much He loves people. He tells Jesus about the huge ditch which separates mankind from God. He explains that Jesus could go to earth and tell mankind about how to get to God. He mimes a cross and explains how Jesus will have to die. Then, He shows how Jesus will come back to life and act as a bridge between the clowns and God. Jesus agrees to the bold plan.

Jesus steps up on the chair and steps across the ditch. The clowns greet him with wonder and excitement. Jesus tells them about God the Father. Some of the clowns get angry. They grab Jesus and take him to the middle of the ditch, between the two chairs. They pretend to nail him to a cross. They hit him and spit on him. Jesus suffers on the cross and dies. The clowns turn their backs on him. God watches, and after a pause, God blows life back into His Son. Jesus rises from the dead. He is victorious! Jesus calls to the clowns and he tells them that they can now get into heaven.

Jesus acts as a bridge as each clown steps across the chairs in order to get to God. Jesus helps them across the great divide of sin. The clowns hug God when they arrive in heaven. Everyone celebrates.

Narrator: *Jesus is the only way to get to God. It was impossible for man to get to God by himself, so God sent His only Son, Jesus Christ, to earth to tell us how we could make it to heaven to be with God. Some people hated Jesus, and they nailed Him to a cross. Jesus died, but on the third day, God raised Him from the dead. Now, Jesus is the bridge to heaven. He said, "I am the way, the truth, and the life, no one comes to the Father except through Me."*

Jesus will forgive you of your sins and He will help you get to God. Will you make Jesus the Lord of your life?

Clown Skit #3: The Bumblebee Game

This is an old vaudevillian skit. It makes a great icebreaker at the beginning of the show. Here is the version Feliz and Gozo perform.

Props: Two cups of water. One should be hidden on stage and one should be placed in the back of the room.

Feliz: Hey, Gozo! Would you like to play a game?

Gozo: Wow! I love games. What kind of game are we going to play?

Feliz: This is a special game.

Gozo: Are we going to play football?

Feliz: No! There's no room in here to play football. Besides, no one here likes football.

Audience: Yes we do.

Gozo: (Gozo lists a bunch of different games and each time Feliz

shakes his head "no.") Let's play basketball...golf...soccer...badminton...volleyball...chess...checkers...Monopoly...marbles...

Feliz: No. This is a special game. I call it the Bumblebee Game.

Gozo: Oh boy...oh boy... What's the Bumblebee Game?

Feliz: Don't tell me you've never heard of the Bumblebee Game.

Gozo: I've never heard of the Bumblebee Game.

Feliz: I told you not to tell me that. Now, here's how the game works. I get to be the queen bee and you get to be the worker bee and you have to do everything I tell you to do.

Gozo: Wait a minute! Why can't I be the queen bee and you be the worker bee, and you do everything I tell you to do?

Feliz: Because the audience wants ME to be the queen bee.

Audience: No we don't. We want Gozo to be the queen bee.

Gozo: Ha, Ha. I get to be the queen bee. Now, what do I have to do?

Feliz: First, you say "Feliz...Go get me some honey." Then I go get you some honey and when I come back, you say "Feliz...Did you get the honey?" And I say, "Hummm...Hum," but I need the whole audience to help me. Everyone say "Hummm...Hum."

Audience: Hummm...Hum.

Feliz: Then you say "Then give it to me!" Are you ready to play?

Gozo: Yes. Here we go. Feliz...Go get me some honey.

(Feliz buzzes off, buzzes a few people, flies back to the back of the room and takes a drink from the glass. He keeps the water in his mouth and the buzz becomes a hum as he flies back up front.)

Gozo: Did you get the honey?

Feliz: (He motions to the audience to get their help as he says), "Hummm...Hum."

Gozo: Then, give it to me!

(Feliz spits the water all over Gozo.)

Feliz: I love this game! Everyone stand up, we are going to sing a song.

Gozo: No, we are not. Everyone sit back down. Feliz, we are going to play a game.

Feliz: No, I don't think we have time.

Gozo: Yes we do. This is a special game.

Feliz: Let's play basketball, football, tennis, chess, checkers...tiddlywinks.

Gozo: No, we are going to play the Bumblebee game.

(Feliz tries to run off the stage but Gozo grabs him and forces him to sit down in the chair.)

Gozo: This is how it works. You say "Gozo, go get me some honey" and I buzz and get you some honey and you say "Gozo, did you get the honey?" and then I say, "Hummm...Hum" but the whole audience says it with me. Then you say, "Then give it to me," and I give it to you!

Feliz: (Looks scared) Alright...Gozo, go get me some honey."

(Gozo races off towards the back and takes a drink of water. Meanwhile, Feliz has an idea. He spots a glass of water and he slides out of the chair and takes a drink. Most of the audience sees him do this but Gozo does not have a clue, when he arrives back up front, Feliz is sitting in the chair with his cheeks full of water. Gozo tries to get Feliz to say his lines but Feliz just sits there. Gozo gets madder and madder but he can not say anything with his mouth full of water. He starts hopping up and down but Feliz just ignores him. Finally, Gozo swallows the water.)

Gozo: You were supposed to say "Did you get the honey."

(Feliz stands up and the whole audience says with him, "Hummm... Hum.")

Gozo: Then...you were supposed to say, "Then give it to me."

(Feliz turns and gives it to Gozo again. He spits all over him. The audience roars with laughter.)

Clown Skit #4: The Sad Hobo who Became Happy

Characters: A Hobo clown
              Teacher
              Jesus

Props: A huge dirty laundry bag
Four ugly packages labeled "Hate," Fear," "Anger," and "Sin."
Four beautifully wrapped presents entitled "Love," "Joy," "Peace," and "Forgiveness."
Jesus costume

(A sad hobo clown interrupts the middle of the service. He is making mean faces at kids and trying to take their seats. Over his shoulder is a huge dirty bag that he is lugging around. The person in charge of the service asks the ushers to escort the rude clown outside but the hobo makes lots of noise and fights the ushers. Finally, the head teacher decides to witness to the hobo clown. The hobo is brought up front and he grumpily steals a seat, sits down, and begins to pick his teeth.)

Teacher: Excuse me, sir, could you tell me what's the matter?

Hobo: No!

Teacher: But, we want to help you. Could you tell me what is bothering you?

Hobo: (Snarls) No! Nothing's bothering me.

Teacher: Sir, you are all sad and mad. Why do you have a frown on your face?

Hobo: Go away!

Teacher: (To the boys and girls) Let's try to find out why this man is so sad. Perhaps there is something in his bag which is making him angry. Excuse me, sir, could we look in your bag? Is there something in there that is making you upset?

Hobo: No!

(The teacher tries to peek inside the bag but the Hobo jumps up and hides the bag behind his back. He does not want to give the bag up. The teacher is persistent and finally the Hobo pulls a package out of the bag. In bold letters, the package says "Hate.")

Teacher: Hate! No wonder you are so upset. Give me that. (Hobo has hate written all over his face, but since the teacher is kind and gentle, he slowly hands the "Hate" over.) Boys and girls, we need to get rid of this hate. Did you know that Jesus Christ died on the cross in order to take away our hate? (Jesus comes out on the stage, stretches out His arms, and the teacher hands the hate to Jesus.

Teacher: What else are you hiding in that bag? (Hobo pulls out "Anger." He raises his fist in anger and shakes it at the children.) Boys and girls, this clown has anger in his heart. Only Jesus can take the anger away. Sir, do you want to give your anger to Jesus? (The Hobo hesitantly hands the anger to the teacher who gives it to Jesus.)

Teacher: Is there anything else in your bag? (The Hobo pulls out a package entitled "Fear." He pretends to be afraid and hides behind his bag. But, at the teacher's coaxing he hands the fear over and it is given to Jesus.)

Teacher: It looks like you have one more package in your bag. (The Hobo pulls out "Sin." Quickly, he runs over to Jesus and gives Him the sin. He bows down before Jesus. Then Jesus lifts the Hobo clown up and hugs him. Jesus throws away the four evil packages; hate, anger, fear, and sin. He goes backstage and comes out with beautifully wrapped presents for the Hobo. The presents are "Love," "Joy," "Peace," and "Forgiveness." The Hobo happily accepts the gifts and he walks out hand-in-hand with Jesus.

Teacher: Jesus takes away our fears, our hate, our anger, and our sin; and He replaces these ugly things with love, joy, peace, and forgiveness. Many people are sad because they are carrying around weights and burdens. It is time to give your burdens to the Lord and allow Him to carry them. When you do, He will give you wonderful new gifts! Mr. Hobo is not sad anymore, now we can call him "Happy Hobo."

Clown Skit #5: Do You Have Goodness in your Heart?
Characters: Good Gus
              Bad Bob
              Game Show Host

Props: A good box with a Bible, a heart, a cross, an apple and an orange.
A bad box with a beer, a sign that says hate, a gun, an apple core and a banana peel.

This drama is similar to the last one except that it compares the good with the bad. The scene is a game show. The teacher is the host of the show and two clowns compete for prizes. Use music to set the scene. A buzzer can go off each time a wrong answer is given.

Host: Welcome, ladies and gentlemen, to the game show "Oh, my Goodness," the game show where we discover if you have goodness in your heart...or badness. If you are good, you will get good prizes, but if you are bad, you will receive bad prizes. With us today we have two contestants. Please welcome contestant number one, "Good Gus" and contestant number two, "Bad Bob." I wonder, who is going to win?

The studio audience is going to help us out by being the judges today. If someone has goodness in their heart, I want you to say "DING, DING, DING." But, if someone has badness in their heart, I want you to make this sound, "BZZZZZZZZZ."

Gus, you get to go first. Show us what you have in your heart.

(Gus reaches into his box and pulls out a Bible.)

Host: Audience, is the Bible good or bad? Remember, for good things you say "DING, DING, DING," and for bad things you yell "BZZZZZZZZZ."

Audience: DING, DING, DING

Host: One thousand points for Gus the clown! Now, Bad Bob, could you show us what you have hidden in your heart?

(Bob reaches into his box and pulls out a beer bottle.)

Host: Audience, is this good or bad?

Audience: BZZZZZZZZZ.

Host: Sorry, Mr. Bob, you do not get any points for beer. (Bob looks mad.) Gus, its your turn again. What else do you have in your heart?

(Gus pulls out a bright red heart which represents "Love.")

Host: Audience?

Audience: DING, DING, DING.

Host: Another thousand points for Good Gus. Mr. Bob, what can you show us? (Bob pulls out a dirty sign that says "Hate.")

Audience: BZZZZZZZZZ.

Host: I'm sorry, but hate is not good. Gus, what else do you have?

(Gus pulls out a cross.)

Audience: DING, DING, DING.

Host: Bad Bob, do you have anything to match a cross.

(Bad Bob grabs a toy gun and starts threatening children with it.)

Audience: BZZZZZZZZZ.

Host: The score is three thousand points for Good Gus and zero for Bad Bob. Now for our bonus round. I am going to ask a question and we'll see which one of you answers it best. (The host opens up an envelope and reads the bonus question.) Do you have any of the fruit of the Spirit in your life?

(Good Gus reaches into his box and withdraws an apple and an orange. Bad Bob reaches into his box and removes a rotten apple core and a banana peel.)

Host: It looks like Good Gus is the winner! I'm sorry, Bad Bob, but it looks like you are the loser. The prize for Gus comes straight from God and it is..."Life!" And Bad Bob gets... "Death."

(Bad Bob looks sad and the game show host takes pity on him.)

Host: Bad Bob, you do not want death as a prize, do you? (Bob shakes his head "No.") Well, you can have good things in your heart if you ask forgiveness for all your sins and invite Jesus into your heart. Jesus will give you all kinds of good things. Pray this prayer with me. "Jesus, please come into my heart. I am sorry for all the wrong things I have done. Please, forgive me. Fill my life full of blessings. Amen." Now we will call you "Blessed Bob."

Clown Skit #6: Gymnastic Routine
A clown runs out on stage and announces that he is going to stand on only one finger. After lots of warm up, the clown puts his finger down on the ground and steps on it.

Clown Skit #7: The Endless Rope
A clown appears and announces that there is nothing up his sleeve. As he rolls up his sleeves to prove it, he discovers the end of a rope up one sleeve. He begins to pull it out. More and more comes until he tugs and it won't come anymore. He lifts up his left pant leg to discover that the rope is tied to his left ankle. Then he stoops down and pulls the rope out from his right ankle. In other words, the audience has seen three ends to the same rope. Finally, he pulls and pulls until the entire rope comes out and tied to a fourth end is his pair of heart covered underwear.

Clown Skit #8: The Straitjacket Escape
One clown is tied up with ropes and put into a straitjacket. Another clown is blindfolded with his hands crossed over his chest. The

blindfolded clown counts backwards from thirty and when he reaches zero, he is going to fall straight backwards and trust his friend to catch him. Of course, the friend must struggle to get free from the straightjacket in time to catch the other clown. The straightjacket represents sin. If we are caught up in sin, it is extremely difficult to help our friends when they are in trouble.

Clown Skit #9: All Mixed Up

A group of clowns walks unto the stage. Each clown has a large sign with a letter. After a lot of fumbling around and frustration as they try to figure out what the letters say, they line up in the proper order so the audience can read the message. Possible messages could be: "God is Good," or "Jesus Loves You."

A Complete Clown Program

Don't Mess with Sin

In the next few pages, I am going to give you an entire program you can perform as a clown. This program is versatile; you can perform it with two clowns or with many clowns. Each component works separately, but when you present all of them in one program, it emphasizes the importance of not touching sin. The reason we hit this theme from so many angles in one program is because the more times you say something, the longer the children will remember what you said.

We know this program works because we have used these routines hundreds of times. Every time we teach children not to mess with sin, many get saved! This program has been tried, tested, evaluated, rewritten, tried again, and polished. Now, I am going to give you the words to say, and the keys to timing, and everything else you need to make this program work for your group.

Intro

Introduce the clowns who are performing and do an icebreaker named, The Colored Square Game. This is an awesome icebreaker and it quickly involves the entire audience. The game is simple. It involves five large colored cards. Each card is a different color, and

requires a different action from the children. Here is an example of some of the possible actions.

1. Red Card - Everyone shouts "Praise the Lord."
2. Green Card - Everyone shouts "Hallelujah."
3. Orange Card - Everyone claps.
4. Blue Card - Everyone stands up and sits back down.
5. Purple Card - Everyone scratches the back of the person next to them.

The teacher holds the five cards in his hand. Every time the teacher raises one of the cards above his head, the children must perform the correct action. The fun comes from the children attempting to quickly remember what action each card requires.

You can give a prize to the first person to do the appropriate action when each card is raised or you can give points to which ever team does the right action first.

Songs

Sing songs which have lots of actions. All the clowns can help the kids learn the actions. When you sing worship songs, you can teach the children the sign language for the song. Doing actions helps children concentrate on worshiping God.

Sample Songs:
1. Father Abraham
2. If you are saved and you know it, clap your hands
3. God is so Good

Juggling

Put on some circus music and all the clowns who know how to juggle can entertain the audience. Or you can tell a story using juggling props or be creative. This is a great time to do gymnastics, string figures, a balloon animal who does tricks, or a puppet skit.

Drama - The Sin Chair

Props Needed:
Chair
Sign - one side says "Do Not Touch" and the other side says "Sin"

Characters:
One mother clown
A clown who pretends to be a young disobedient boy.

Action: The scene opens with the chair in the middle of the stage. The sign is attached to the chair and it says "Do Not Touch."

The two clowns are walking along and they see the chair. Immediately, the young clown tries to sit down in the chair but at the last moment, his mother grabs him. She tells him not to touch the chair. He rebelliously tries to touch the chair but again, she grabs him. She explains that he is not allowed to touch the chair. She can even point to the sign and get the whole audience to read the sign together, "Do Not Touch." The baby clown repeats it. He mimes that he will not touch the chair.

His mother has to go run an errand. As she leaves, she asks the audience to let her know if her son touches the chair. He points to the chair and mimes that he will not touch it while she is gone. She waves at him and he waves back as she leaves. (She steps offstage for a moment.)

As soon as his mom is gone, he starts looking longingly at the chair. He moves closer and closer to the chair. Finally, he sticks out one finger and slowly begins to move it towards the chair. The audience screams at him not to touch it and he tries to get them to be quiet so his mom will not hear. He repeats this several times until finally, he

reaches out and touches the chair with one finger. Nothing happens. He touches it again. He slaps it with his palm and shows the audience that nothing happened. Finally, he puts one hand on the back of chair and leans on it. After a little bit, he tries to take his hand off, but the hand is stuck. He begins to struggle with the chair but his hand will not come off.

Just as he is frantically trying to get unstuck, his mother comes back. She looks at him sadly and waves at him. The young clown quickly leans nonchalantly on the chair, crosses his legs, and waves back. She leaves the stage again and he frantically tries to get free again. In the process, he puts his other hand on the front of the chair and this hand gets stuck, too.

His mother comes back and waves. He tries to pretend that nothing is wrong and he waves back with one foot. She leaves and he puts one foot in the middle of the chair to try to push it off his hands. Of course the foot gets stuck. Mom comes and waves and he waves with the other foot. After she is gone again, he manages to get his other foot stuck on the chair. He bounces around for a minute in a ridiculous situation.

His mom returns for the last time and waves. He has nothing left to wave. He tries to shake his head and wave his tongue but this does not appear to work. His mom is still waving so he scoots his chair around in a circle, turning his rear towards the audience and waves his posterior at the audience. (This is a great visual punch line to this skit. Waving is a running gag which happens every time the mom comes out. Once he gets stuck, the audience is wondering how he is going to wave, and this solution to the problem is hilarious.)

The clown is obviously in a lot of trouble. The mom wonders what

she can do to rescue her son. Finally, she has an idea. She will pray. She gets down on her knees and begins to pray. As she does, her son slowly becomes unglued from the chair. By the time she is finished praying, he has become completely unstuck and he is kneeling next to her. They stand up and hug.

The mom goes over to the chair and carefully takes the sign off. She gets the audience to say, "Do Not Touch." Then she turns the sign over to reveal that it says "SIN" on the other side. She has the whole audience say "Do Not Touch Sin." After this she can begin teaching her son, and the audience, what sin is, and why we need to stay away from it.

Teach a Memory Verse

"If we confess our sins, He is faithful to forgive us our sins..." (1 John 1:9). Write this verse on six large pieces of posterboard. Ask the children to repeat the verse repeatedly until they can say it from memory. Reward children with candy for saying the verse without any mistakes.

Illustration - God will wash away sins

Props: This is a trick so you will need to make several specialized props.

1. You will need a soap box which falls apart. Find a soap box and empty it. Now, carefully take it apart along the seams until it can lie flat. Put it back together, using velcro to hold it together instead of glue. It should completely fall apart when the velcro is pulled apart.

2. You will need a white handkerchief, folded in half diagonally corner to corner and sewed up along the edge. Inside this handkerchief is a tube which is tied with a string to the top corner.

3. Two normal clean handkerchiefs.

4. Write "Lying," "Cheating," and "Stealing," in large letters with

black ink on three more handkerchiefs.

The basic idea of this trick is simple.

Step #1: Show the kids three dirty handkerchiefs.

Step #2: Put the handkerchiefs inside the soap box. Actually, they go into the tube inside the fake handkerchief.

Step #3: Pretend to wash the handkerchiefs. A washing machine has three cycles. The wash cycle (shake the box), the spin cycle (spin around in circles), and the rinse cycle (pretend to spit into the box).

Step #4: Turn the box upside down (this is the main misdirection involved in the trick) and begin to pull out the clean handkerchiefs which were already planted inside the box. Pull out the first two and show them to be completely clean. Pull out the third handkerchief (the one with the dirty handkerchiefs hidden inside). Put all three handkerchiefs away, out of sight.

Step #5: The children think they have caught you because they saw you turn the box upside down. They begin to yell at you to show them the inside of the box. You appear to be hesitant, but finally you pull the entire box apart and clearly prove that the dirty handkerchiefs are now clean.

Action: The trick begins with one clown holding the three dirty handkerchiefs. The box of soap has three clean handkerchiefs folded up inside of it. Two of the handkerchiefs are normal but the third one is sewed up along one edge and there is a tube hidden inside which has enough room for the dirty handkerchiefs to be hidden inside of it.

Clown #1: Boys and Girls, I hope you do not mind, but I brought with me today some of my dirty laundry. (Hold up the first handkerchief.) What does this say? It says "Lying." Is lying good? Does God like lying? In fact, the Bible says, "Thou shalt not lie." We need to wash this sin off this dirty handkerchief. To accomplish that we

need a washing machine. (Clown #1 asks Clown #2: "Did you bring the washing machine like I told you?")

Clown #2: Washing machine?

Clown #1: Do not tell me you forgot the washing machine.

Clown #2: Uhh...I forgot the washing machine.

Clown #1: I told you not to tell me that. Now how in the world are we supposed to wash my handkerchiefs?

Clown #2: I could be the washing machine.

Clown #1: You can't be a washing machine. You do not even know what a washing machine does, besides you don't have any soap.

Clown #2: I know what a machine does...and I have soap. (Clown #2 holds up a box of soap.) I have Tide...with bleach.

Clown #1: Well, I guess you can try to clean this handkerchief but I do not think it will work. (He hands the handkerchief that says "Lying" to the second clown.)

Clown #2: (He puts the handkerchief inside the box of soap. In reality, it goes into the tube which is hidden inside the third white handkerchief.)

Clown #1: (Hold up the second dirty handkerchief.) What does this say? Stealing! Is stealing good? No. In fact, the Bible says "Thou shalt not _____. We need to clean this up, don't we boys and girls? (He hands the stealing handkerchief to the second clown who puts it inside the Tide box.) (Hold up the third handkerchief.) What

does this say? Cheating! Does God like cheating? What about just a little tiny bit of cheating? (Children yell "No!") Let's clean this dirty handkerchief up. (Hands third dirty handkerchief to his partner.) Did you know that sin is dirty? When we do something that God does not like, it is like falling into a mud puddle. When you get dirt on yourself, you have to use soap to get cleaned up. When you sin, you need the power of God to help you get cleaned up. (Clown 2 is finished putting the handkerchiefs inside the tube inside the box.) How in the world do you think you are going to clean those things?

Clown#2: I already told you...I am going to pretend to be a washing machine. I know exactly what a washing machine does. It has cycles. First, there is a wash cycle (he jumps up and down a dozen times), next there is a spin cycle (he spins around and around), then there is a rinse cycle (he lifts up the lid of the box and pretends to spit into the box). Now, they are all clean!

Clown #1: Let me see. (Grab the box, turn it upside down, reach in, and pull out the first clean handkerchief.) Wow! It's all clean. (Pull out the second one and show both sides.) This one is all clean too. (Pull out the one with the dirty handkerchiefs inside. Briefly show it to the audience, put it behind the other handkerchiefs, and put all three of them out of sight. (If you have done this correctly, the audience will think the dirty handkerchiefs are still in the box. This is why this trick is so brilliant, you sneak the dirty handkerchiefs out right underneath the noses of the audience while they are suspecting the box of trickery. They will begin to yell for you to show them the box.)

Clown #2: Let me see the box. Wow. It's empty! (Of course, the audience does not believe it. They will demand to see for themselves.)

Clown #1: (Looks in the soap box.) Yes. It's empty. What? You

don't believe us? Do you think we would lie to you? But, we just told you not to lie. Alright, I will show you the box. You'll are too smart for us. (Undo the velcro on the box so the entire thing falls apart. The audience can clearly see that it is impossible for anything to have been inside. They sit stunned since they were so sure they figured the trick out. They thought they caught you but you actually hoodwinked them.)

Clown #2: Boys and girls, God washes away our sins and gives us nice, white, clean hearts. Let's give Him a great, big hand!

Teaching - The Monkey Trap

Props: First, you will need to make a monkey trap. You will need an envelope box with a hole cut in the top. The hole is big enough for someone to put their hand in, but once they grab the bait, it is small enough that they can not get their hand out. Cover the entire box with duct tape so it looks like a trap and attach a long rope to one corner.
Banana
Actors: One clown does the teaching
 A second clown pretends to be a monkey

Action:
Boys and Girls, I would like to tell you a story. How many of you know where South America is? Did you know that way down in the bottom of South America, there are monkeys? That's right, and there are also monkey hunters. When the monkey hunters want to catch the monkeys, they take a box just like this box, and they cut a hole in the top.

Then they put some bait inside the trap to attract the monkeys. What kind of bait do you think they use to catch monkeys? (Wait for children to say "Bananas.") That's right, monkeys love bananas! (Place

the banana inside the trap.) The monkey hunters put the banana inside the trap and then they tie the trap to a tree.

The monkeys are smart. They know the banana is in a trap and they stay as far away from it as possible. They know if they put their hands inside the box, they will be trapped. But, there is always a stupid monkey who comes and starts sniffing the banana.

That's right, a stupid monkey ... (Second clown enters from the back acting like a stupid monkey by making sounds like a monkey, by picking fleas out of kids hair, and by beating on his chest. He says, "Hoo, ha, ha, hoo, eee, ha, hoo, ha, ha.")

The stupid monkey smells the banana and he wants the banana. He looks all over until he spots the trap. He begins touching and playing with the trap. He sniffs at the banana and finally he reaches into the trap and grabs the bait.

The stupid monkey tries to get the banana out of the trap but the hole is too small. He tries to walk away but he can not because the trap is tied to the tree. The poor, stupid monkey is trapped. Now, boys and girls, what does the monkey have to do to get out of the trap? (Wait for the children to say "Let go of the banana.") That's right! All the monkey has to do to get out of the trap is let go of the banana. But, the monkey is so stupid that he will hold onto the banana until the monkey hunters come and capture him.

Boys and girls, this monkey trap reminds me of another kind of trap. Sin is exactly like this trap. Sin might look good, but if you reach out and grab sin, it will trap you. Some people think they can play with sin without getting caught, but sin will trap you every time.

The good news is that you can be set free from the trap of sin. If you

pray to God and ask forgiveness for your sins, He will set you set you free from every wrong thing you have ever done.

Hey, stupid monkey, do you want to become a smart monkey by praying and asking for God to help you get out of this trap? (Monkey shakes his head yes.)

Pray this prayer with the monkey. Dear God, please help this monkey let go of sin. He does not want to be trapped. He believes Jesus died on the cross so he could be set free from the trap of sin. In the name of Jesus, Amen. (As the prayer is said, the monkey lets go of the trap and it drops to the floor. The monkey gets excited and jumps around.) Let's give this monkey a round of applause because Jesus has set him free! Now, he is a very smart monkey.

Altar Call
Give the children an opportunity to accept Jesus as their Lord and Savior. Explain that everyone sins, and this sin traps us. If we invite Jesus into our lives, He frees us from the trap of sin.

Ask everyone to close their eyes and lead them in this prayer. "Dear God, I am sorry for all the wrong things I have done. I am sorry for lying, cheating, stealing, and disobeying. Please forgive me. Jesus, I believe You are the Son of God and I invite You into my life. I will serve You forever. Amen."

Ask the children to draw a door on their hearts. Draw a doorknob. Open the door and say, "Jesus, come in today, come in to stay. Amen." Tell the children that Jesus will never leave them nor forsake them so they will never need to open that door again. Close the door and pull out a key. Lock the door and on the count of three throw the key as far as you possibly can.

Ending Song

We usually end with this song. We ask the children to help us create a rhythm by repeatedly slapping their legs twice and then clapping once.

Jesus loves me this I know
for the Bible tells me so.
Little ones to Him belong,
in Christ Jesus we are strong.

Jesus loves me when I'm good,
when I do the things I should,
Jesus loves me when I'm bad,
though it makes Him very sad.
(Repeat chorus)

We're the Clowns for Christ
and we are serving God's Son
We're glad you all made it,
and I hope that you had fun!
(Repeat chorus)

Clown Ministry
Resource List

Fife, Bruce. *Creative Clowning*. Colorado Springs, CO: Piccadilly Books. 1992. - This is the single best guide to clowning available. It is a must for anyone starting a clown group. It includes ideas on make-up, comedy, juggling, balloon animals, unicycles, costumes, and everything else.

Fife, Bruce. *How to be a Goofy Juggler*. Colorado Springs, CO: Piccadilly Books. 1989. - Lots of fun juggling tricks and jokes. Quite a bit of the material can be used by a juggler or non-juggler.

Litherland, Janet. *The Clown Ministry Handbook*. Colorado Springs, CO: Meriwether Publishing, 1989. - This is a great beginning guide for using clowns in ministry. Lot's of great skit ideas.

McVicar, Wes. *Clown Act Omnibus*. Colorado Springs, CO: Meriwether Publishing, 1987. - This book has almost one hundred skits for clowns to perform.

Moss, Larry. *Twisting History: Lessons in Balloon Sculpturing*. Rochester, NY: Fooled Ya.1995.- This book teaches some

basic balloon animals.

Shaffer, Floyd. *Clown Ministry*. Loveland, CO: Group Books, 1984. - This book is the classic on Christian Clowning.

Schindler, George. *Basic Balloon Sculpture*. Brooklyn, New York: Show-Biz Services. 1983. - More basic animal balloon material.

For make-up, props, juggling items, balloons, or books call: Top Hat Magic and Costumes. http://www.tophatmagic.com (918) 663-5550

Final Note

Once upon a time, there was a juggler who lived in a land far, far away. He happened to be one of the best jugglers in the whole world and he heard that good jugglers could make a bunch of money if they came to the United States. So, he got on a boat and came across the ocean to America.

When he arrived, he began to juggle on the street corner. First, he would juggle three balls, then he would juggle five balls, then he would juggle clubs and finally he juggled three burning torches high into the air. Everyone loved him and they would clap for him. After they clapped, they would throw money.

The juggler carefully saved every penny. He worked for several years and he became rich. After he had worked hard and earned lots of money, he decided to return to the country he had come from, but he had a problem. In his country, they did not take dollars so he had no way to take his money home.

Until, one day he saw a big beautiful diamond sitting in the window of a store. He entered the store and asked, "How much does the diamond cost?" They named a figure and the juggler had just

enough money to buy it. They put it in a box and the juggler carefully guarded the box because it represented everything he had in the whole world.

He bought a ticket on a ship going home. On the ship, someone recognized him and exclaimed, "Hey, you are one of the best jugglers in the whole world, aren't you?" He proudly told them, "No, I am not one of the best; I am the best juggler in the world!"

They did not believe them so he pulled out his juggling balls and began to juggle. He performed every trick he knew, but they were not impressed. So, he said, "I will throw this juggling ball as high as I can and when it comes down, I will catch it and keep juggling and that will prove that I am the best juggler in the world." But, it did not impress them, so he threw the ball even higher and it still did not impress them.

In a desperate effort to impress the people on the ship, the juggler pulled the box with the jewel out of his pocket and said, "To prove that my skill is greater then any other juggler, I will throw this precious diamond as high as I can, and when it comes down I will juggle it." The passengers replied, "Yes, that would be impressive."

The juggler drew his arm back and threw the diamond as high as he could. Right as it began to come down, the ship hit a wave, and when the ship hit a wave, the juggler's feet slipped, and as the diamond fell, he reached out for it, but it dropped right between his fingers, hit the deck and slowly rolled underneath the rail and into the sea. The juggler lost everything he owned that day because he was foolish.

In this book, I have given you some valuable information on starting a clown ministry, I exhort you, do not drop the ball.

Our Goal?
Every Soul!

Daniel & Jessica King

KING
MINISTRIES
INTERNATIONAL

About the Author

Daniel King and his wife Jessica met in the middle of Africa while they were both on a mission trip. They are in high demand as speakers at churches and conferences all over North America. Their passion, energy, and enthusiasm are enjoyed by audiences everywhere they go.

They are international missionary evangelists who do massive soul-winning festivals in countries around the world. Their passion for the lost has taken them to over sixty nations preaching the gospel to crowds that often exceed 50,000 people.

Daniel was called into the ministry when he was five years old and began to preach when he was six. His parents became missionaries to Mexico when he was ten. When he was fourteen he started a children's ministry that gave him the opportunity to minister in some of America's largest churches while still a teenager.

At the age of fifteen, Daniel read a book where the author encouraged young people to set a goal to earn $1,000,000. Daniel reinterpreted the message and determined to win 1,000,000 people to Christ every year.

Daniel has authored ten books including his best sellers *Healing Power*, *The Secret of Obed-Edom*, and *Fire Power*. His book *Welcome to the Kingdom* has been given away to tens of thousands of new believers.

Soul Winning Festivals

Metu, Ethiopia

Khushpur, Pakistan

Roca Blanca, Mexico

Sialkot, Pakistan

Agere Maryam, Ethiopia

Kisaran, Indonesia

Brazil

Haiti

Pakistan

Indonesia

India

Haiti

South Africa

Columbia

Peru

Nicaragua

THE Million Heirs Club

When Daniel King was fifteen years old, he set a goal to lead 1,000,000 people to Jesus before his 30th birthday. Instead of trying to become a millionaire, he decided to lead a million "heirs" into the kingdom of God. *"If you belong to Christ then you are heirs"* (Galatians 3:29).

After celebrating the completion of this goal, Daniel & Jessica made it their mission to go for one million souls every year.

This **Quest for Souls** is accomplished through:
* Soul Winning Festivals
* Leadership Training
* Literature Distribution
* Humanitarian Relief

Would you help us lead
people to Jesus by joining
The MillionHeir's Club?

Visit www.kingministries.com to get involved!

THE SECRET OF OBED-EDOM

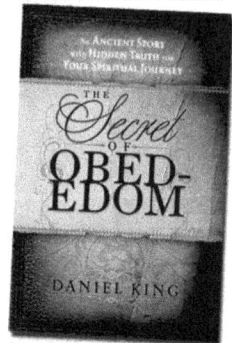

Unlock the secret to supernatural promotion and a more intimate walk with God. Unleash amazing blessing in your life!

$20.00

MOVE

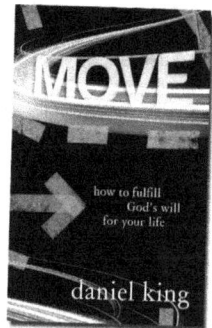

What is God's will for your life? Learn how to find and fulfill your destiny.

$10.00

POWER OF FASTING

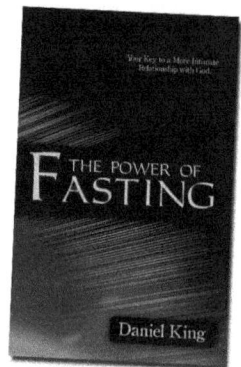

Discover deeper intimacy with God and unleash the answer to your prayers.

$10.00

KING MINISTRIES INTERNATIONAL

TOLL FREE: 1-877-431-4276
PO Box 701113
TULSA, OK 74170 USA

ORDER ONLINE:
WWW.KINGMINISTRIES.COM

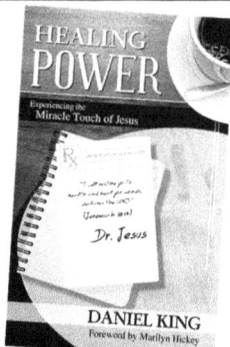

The vision of King Ministries is to lead 1,000,000 people to Jesus every year and to train believers to become leaders.

To contact Daniel & Jessica King:

Write:
King Ministries International
PO Box 701113
Tulsa, OK 74170 USA

King Ministries Canada
PO Box 3401
Morinville, Alberta T8R 1S3 Canada

Call toll-free:
1-877-431-4276

Visit us online:
www.kingministries.com

E-Mail:
daniel@kingministries.com

www.ingramcontent.com/pod-product-compliance
Lightning Source LLC
Chambersburg PA
CBHW072009060426
42446CB00042B/2265